YOUR KNOWLEDGE HAS VALUE

- We will publish your bachelor's and master's thesis, essays and papers

- Your own eBook and book - sold worldwide in all relevant shops

- Earn money with each sale

Upload your text at www.GRIN.com
and publish for free

Matthias Beer

Monetary Policy in Brazil

GRIN Verlag

Bibliografische Information der Deutschen Nationalbibliothek:

Die Deutsche Bibliothek verzeichnet diese Publikation in der Deutschen National-
bibliografie; detaillierte bibliografische Daten sind im Internet über http://dnb.d-
nb.de/ abrufbar.

Dieses Werk sowie alle darin enthaltenen einzelnen Beiträge und Abbildungen
sind urheberrechtlich geschützt. Jede Verwertung, die nicht ausdrücklich vom
Urheberrechtsschutz zugelassen ist, bedarf der vorherigen Zustimmung des Verla-
ges. Das gilt insbesondere für Vervielfältigungen, Bearbeitungen, Übersetzungen,
Mikroverfilmungen, Auswertungen durch Datenbanken und für die Einspeicherung
und Verarbeitung in elektronische Systeme. Alle Rechte, auch die des auszugsweisen
Nachdrucks, der fotomechanischen Wiedergabe (einschließlich Mikrokopie) sowie
der Auswertung durch Datenbanken oder ähnliche Einrichtungen, vorbehalten.

Imprint:

Copyright © 2011 GRIN Verlag GmbH
Druck und Bindung: Books on Demand GmbH, Norderstedt Germany
ISBN: 978-3-656-49558-1

This book at GRIN:

http://www.grin.com/en/e-book/233262/monetary-policy-in-brazil

GRIN - Your knowledge has value

Der GRIN Verlag publiziert seit 1998 wissenschaftliche Arbeiten von Studenten, Hochschullehrern und anderen Akademikern als eBook und gedrucktes Buch. Die Verlagswebsite www.grin.com ist die ideale Plattform zur Veröffentlichung von Hausarbeiten, Abschlussarbeiten, wissenschaftlichen Aufsätzen, Dissertationen und Fachbüchern.

Visit us on the internet:

http://www.grin.com/

http://www.facebook.com/grincom

http://www.twitter.com/grin_com

Monetary Policy in Brazil

Master of Business Administration (MBA)

Semester:	WS2010
Module:	Economics
Authors:	Matthias Beer
Place, Date:	Munich, 14. February 2011

Executive Summary

Brazil is the largest country in South America with the highest population. Since 2003, Brazil has improved its macroeconomic stability and built-up foreign reserves. They have further reduced debt and managed to keep inflation rates under control while committing to fiscal responsibilities. Nevertheless, back in history, from the 1960s to 1990s the country was struggling with continuously high inflation rates until Fernando Henrique Cardoso, the minister of finance and later president of Brazil, introduced the "Plano Real" 1st of March 1994.

The assignment describes the financial history of Brazil between the 1960s and 2000 in brief by giving some numbers about inflation rates and highlighting potential reasons for the long period and high rates. The work describes further on the stabilization efforts in the 1990s in Brazil by introducing the "Plano Real", explaining the idea of introducing the Unidade Real de Valor, a parallel, virtual and relative currency to the Cruzeiro Real. In the third chapter the economical relation between money supply and inflation is explained by the quantity theory of money and an alternative to express inflation, the quantity equation, is given. The last part of the essay explains the classical dichotomy in economics in general and analyses the economical data of Brazil for the 1990s in this regards. The assignment is concluded by the ITM checklist.

Table of Contents

Executive Summary I
List of Abbreviations III
List of Figures IV
List of Tables IV
1. Introduction 5
2. Brazils Monetary Stabilization Efforts in the 1990s 6
3. Analysis of Relation between Money Supply and Inflation 7
4. Dichotomy of Economy 9
5. ITM Checklist 11
Bibliography 13

List of Abbreviations

CR   Cruzeiro Real

GDP Gross Domestic Product

ITM Integral Total Management

URV Unidade Real de Valor

USD United States Dollar

List of Figures

Figure 1: Brazil's Inflation Rate 1970 to 1989 (Roberto F. Iunes, 1993, p.38).... 5
Figure 2: Quantity theory of Money (Mankiw, 2001, p.639) 8
Figure 3: Brazil Economy Data 1991 – 2000 10

List of Tables

Equation 1: Quantity Equation 9

1. Introduction

An accumulated inflation rate of 1,000,000,000,000,000% (one quadrillion percent) between 1994 and 1994 was calculated for Brazil by Joelmir Beting in 1996[1].

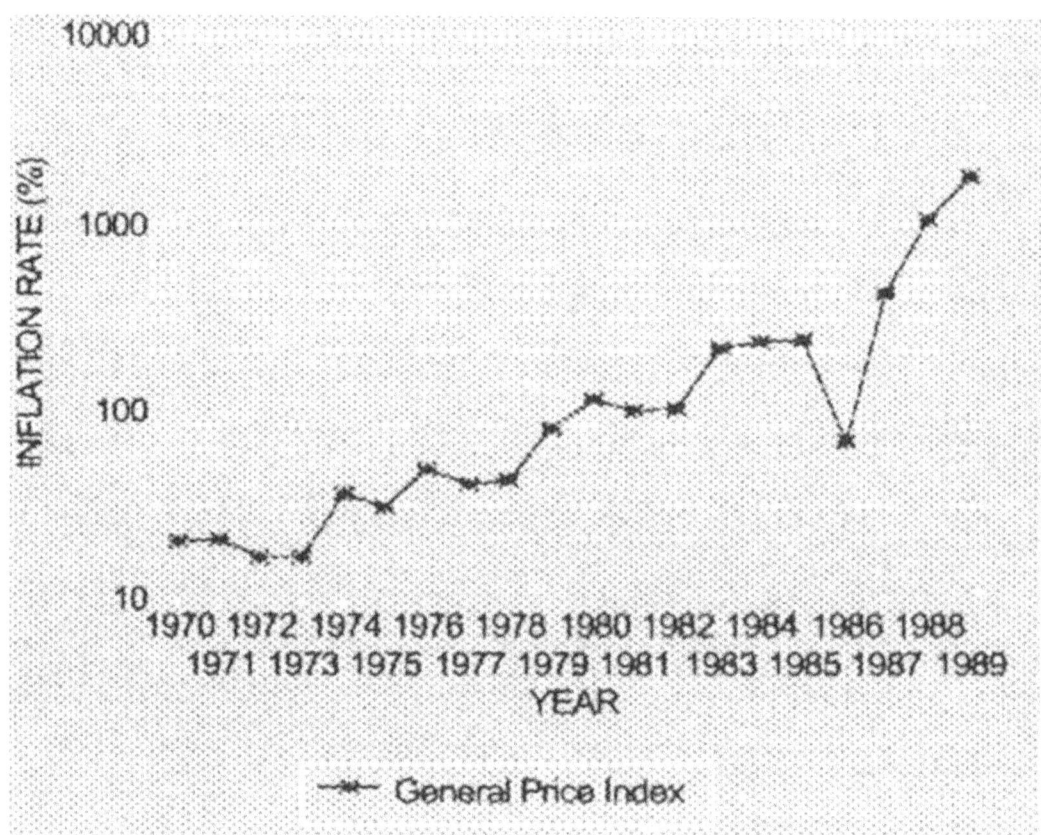

Figure 1: Brazil's Inflation Rate 1970 to 1989 (Roberto F. Iunes, 1993, p.38)

The reason for the high inflation and the long period had several reasons but three of them are obvious. Firstly, the inflation was somehow convenient for the government because the money was printed for a relative low cost for the Ministry of Finance due to collection of inflationary taxes. Secondly, the monetary adjustment, money left in the bank was automatically paid interest overnight, protected the savings from inflation and therefore the government did not face too much pressure from the mid- and upper-class to react against.

---

[1] The report was published at VEJA.com for online subscribers only

Thirdly, understanding inflation in a complex country like Brazil and further more finding appropriate counteractive measures is a highly sophisticated task were many of the best economist of Brazil were involved without success until 1994. In 1994, after several initiatives, the financial minister of Brazil introduced the "Plano Real". The plan brought economical stability to Brazil and enabled to keep up economic growth through the last decade.

2. Brazils Monetary Stabilization Efforts in the 1990s

In the 1990s Fernando Henrique Cardoso, the minister of finance and later president of Brazil, introduced the "Plano Real" 1st of March 1994 with the objective to stabilize the economy. The basic idea of "Plano Real" was to incorporate into international economy by stabilizing the currency and initiating structural reforms in parallel (Parkin 2010).

In General, keeping relative prices with respect to scare resources, are typically leading to an increase in productive investments consequently building the fundamental for an economical recovery. Further on, opening the domestic market for international capital usually brings international technologies as well which are speeding up the process in addition (Bain 2003).

The "Plano Real" was quite successful in stabilizing the currency, neither prices nor savings were frozen but the inflation index was used to create a new non-monetary reference currency, referring to as "Unidade Real de Valor" (URV), within a well prepared change process. The idea behind the new parallel currency to the "Cruzeiro Real" (CR) was to be independent from the inflation by aligning prices to the USD. All goods were priced in both currencies but still had to be paid in CRs. The URV prices were constant over time whereas the others changed on a daily bases (Plano Real 10.01.2011).

The goal of establishing a fictive currency was to unbias people from their expectation in daily raising prices by giving them fixed ones as a reference which leaded after some time also to stable CR prices. After achieving stable prices the virtual URV was used as basis for a new real currency, referring to as "Real". The "Plano Real" stabilized Brazil's economy in the 1990s and enabled a continuous economical growth.

3. Analysis of Relation between Money Supply and Inflation

A continuous price raise of goods and services is commonly known as inflation which means the buying power of a currency decreases. In general, there's a direct relation between the inflation rate of an economy and the amount of money supplied. The mechanism by which excess money is translated into inflation is as follows. The aggregated demand is raised by spending excess money for goods and services which directly impacts into inflation. Further on, a demand raise of labor directly contributes into a higher demand for goods and services which will again raise salaries and labor costs. The more inelastic an aggregated supply is, the higher the impact in inflation is. On the other hand, an increase in demand of goods and services will lead potentially to higher import rates which has a negative impact in the domestic economy and for this reason reduces the money supply. Even more, increased import rates will raise the money supply of foreign exchange markets and therefore lower the exchange rates and increase the inflation rate again.

In order to explain the relationship between money supply and inflation the quantity theory of money can be used as a first approximation. The theory was developed by economists at the beginning of the twentieth century. In general, the assumption describes how the nominal value of aggregate income is determined as well as the demand for money. The theory provides data in addition about how much money is held for a given amount of aggregated income.

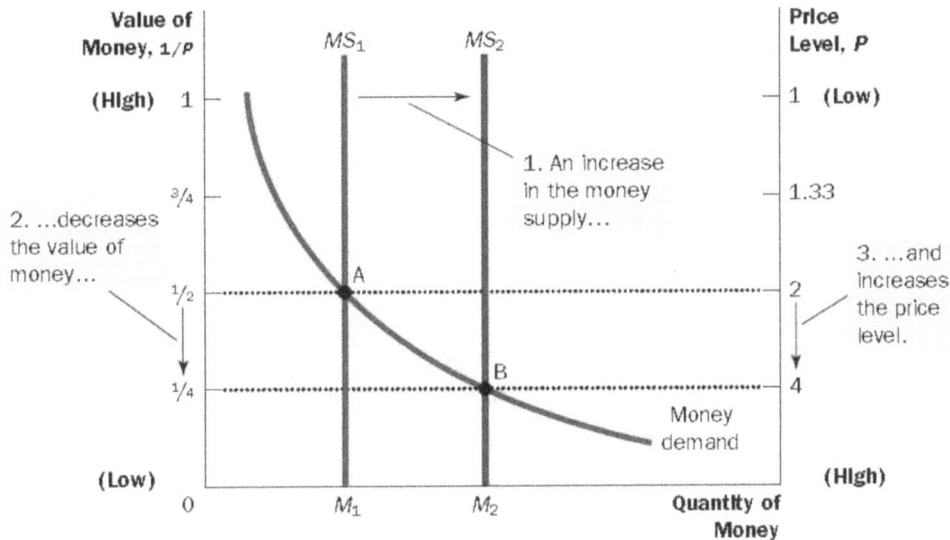

Figure 2: Quantity theory of Money (Mankiw, 2001, p.639)

A typical behavior of an increase in money supply as shown in Figure 2, decreases consequently the value of money and as a result raises the price level of goods and services, commonly known as inflation. In other words, as shown in Figure 2, the point of equilibrium changes from 'A' to 'B' which means and increased money supply reduces the buying power of the currency.

With the theory of money the link between money supply and inflation can be described as follows. A salary increase of 10%, equal a 100 per month, is increasing the buying power at a first glance which means a 10% price increase from 10 to 11 for a certain good or service is probably acceptable but devaluates the buying power. With respect to Figure 2 the money supply goes from MS_1 to MS_2 and consequently the price level P for goods and services increases respectively the value of money 1/P decreases.

As an alternative for the quantity theory of money the quantity equation (Equation 1) can be used. The equation describes the effect the quantity of money has in an economy.

$$M * V = P * Y$$

where M = money supply
V = velocity of circulating money
P = price level
Y = real GDP

Equation 1: Quantity Equation

By solving Equation 1 for V, the velocity of money can be derived. The velocity of money is a measure for how often a bill is used per year to pay goods and services. The velocity of money can be seen as another indicator or metric for the inflation rate of an economy. The more often a bill has to be used, the higher the velocity is, the less busing power the bill has and correspondingly the higher the inflation rate is.

4. Dichotomy of Economy

In economics, dichotomy allows to group economical variables in real and nominal respectively monetary ones. Real, non-monetary variables are for instance output or real interest rates, measured in physical terms whereas nominal variables like for instance money supply or inflation rate are measured in terms of money. According to the classical dichotomy, changes in monetary variables affect other nominal ones but do not affect real values as output, employment or real interest rates. Therefore, money is neutral in a sense that it can not affect real variables. Moreover, in macroeconomics the classical dichotomy refers to the idea that real and nominal variables can be analyzed separately.

An economy exhibits the classical dichotomy if real variables, such as output, unemployment, and real interest rates, can be completely analyzed without considering what is happening to nominal variables. In particular, this means that GDP and other real variables can be determined without knowing the level of the nominal money supply or the rate of inflation.

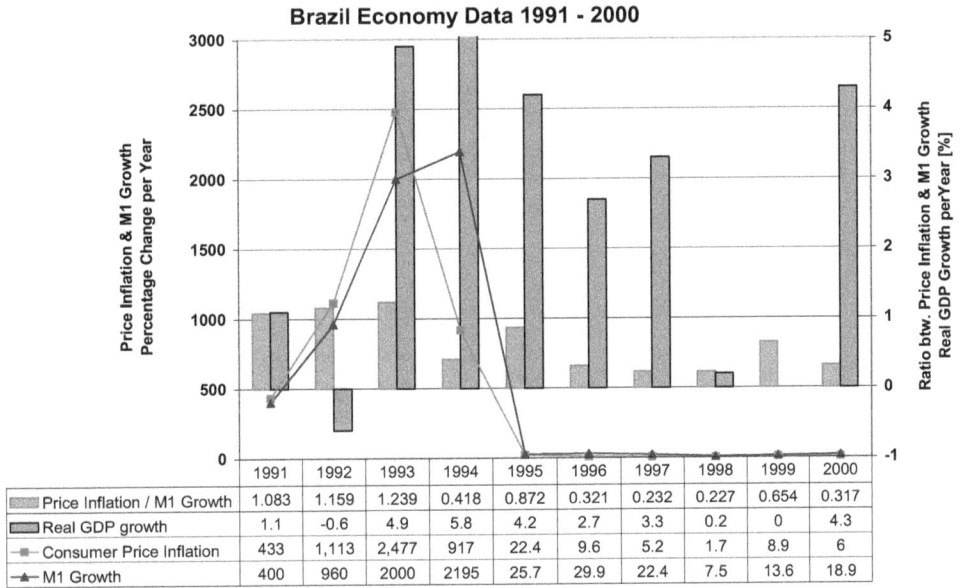

Figure 3: Brazil Economy Data 1991 – 2000

With respect to the economy data of Brazil from the years 1991 to 2000, as shown in Figure 3, one can see that the classical dichotomy does not fully apply. With some exceptions the real GDP growth, illustrated as blue bar in Figure 3, is correlated with the growth of M1, illustrated as blue line in the same diagram. On the other hand, the direct relation between money supply and inflation rate can be seen for the years 1991 to 1993. Starting in 1994, after implementing the "Plano Real" on 1st of March 1994, the behavior changed. The M1 growth was still positive whereas the inflation rate was going down. The relation can also be illustrated by the ratio of both variables which went below 1 in year 1994 and subsequently. Commonly, the classical dichotomy in economics is given for mid- and long terms perspectives but might not always apply for short term considerations as for example in the 1990s in Brazil (Wickens, 2008).

5. ITM Checklist

Complex of Topics	Comments / Suggestions
General Economics	Monetary policy is a versatile topic which requires a holist overview of an economy, about the relations and interaction. Controlling inflation is a part of monetary policy and is usually done by changing the money supply. Commonly, when an economy is trying to lower inflation, central banks will lower lending and at the same time increase interest rates. Vice versa, when inflation drops below a target level, these standards are generally relaxed in order to stimulate the economy. Countries are using their federal banking system usually to set lending and interest limits based on economic data.
Strategic Management	Decisions on the monetary policy of a country require an integral view of an economic situation. Typical approaches like for example control inflation by adjusting lending and interest rates are successful up to a certain extend. High inflation rates or hyperinflation might requiring alternatives such as introducing a virtual currency with fixed relative prices for goods and services in order to unbias people from their expectation in daily raising prices aiming for a stable condition in terms of buying power.
Marketing	Monetary policy consideration with respect to inflation rates has to monitor economical trends and predict future behavior carefully. From a marketing perspective saving and buying activities should be stimulated by certain governmental driven incentives such as special tax benefits or interest rates.

Financial Management	Depending on the economical situation of a country in terms of inflation, certain actions should be considered as counter measures. Besides adjusting rates for loans and interests, variable corporate tax rates can be considered as well to control the GDP assuming nominal and real variables are (partly) correlated.
Human Resources Management	High inflation can cause lay-offs which has in general a negative influence in the economical situation of a country. Counter measures from the government has to be taken and companies has to react sufficiently. A proper HR strategy has to be in place.
Business Law	Monetary policies of countries are complex and considers different aspects from tax regulation to federal banking. All decisions and changes has to be considered and to be in line with respect to given laws and regulations.
Research Methods / Management Decision	Appropriate research methods and models such as the quantity theory of money has to be applied for management decision regarding monetary policy.
Soft Skill / Leadership	Monetary policy decision will mostly face antagonism from parties involved. Diplomatic skills are of importance to communicate and implement changes.

Bibliography

Bain, Keith, and Howells, Peter G. A. *Monetary economics: Policy and its theoretical basis*. Basingstoke, Hampshire: Palgrave Macmillan, 2003. http://www.gbv.de/dms/bowker/toc/9780333792551.pdf.

Duquette, Michel. *Building new democracies: Economic and social reform in Brazil, Chile, and Mexico*. Toronto, Buffalo: University of Toronto Press, 1999. http://www.gbv.de/dms/bowker/toc/9780802044020.pdf.

Giavazzi, Francesco, Goldfajn, Ilan, and Herrera, Santiago. *Inflation targeting, debt, and the Brazilian experience, 1999 to 2003*. Cambridge, Mass.: MIT Press, 2005. http://www.gbv.de/dms/bsz/toc/bsz118183850inh.pdf.

Gwartney, James D. *Economics: Private and public choice*. 12th ed. Mason OH: South-Western Cengage Learning, 2009.

Mankiw, N. G. *Principles of economics*. 2nd ed. Fort Worth, Tex.: Harcourt College Publ., 2001. http://www.gbv.de/dms/hebis-mainz/toc/096129891.pdf.

Parkin, Vincent. *Chronic inflation in an industrializing economy: The Brazilian experience*. Cambridge: Cambridge Univ. Press, 2010. http://www.gbv.de/dms/zbw/614714532.pdf.

"Plano Real - Wikipedia, the free encyclopedia." 2011. http://en.wikipedia.org/wiki/Plano_real, accessed January 2011.

Wickens, Michael. *Macroeconomic theory: A dynamic general equilibrium approach*. Princeton: Princeton Univ. Press, 2008.

Roberto F. Iunes, Carlos A. M. "The Improvement in Child Nutritional Status in Brazil: How did it occur (UNSSCN, 1992, 38 p.): Chapter 1. 1970-1989: A General Picture: Macroeconomic Indicators." 1993.

Lightning Source UK Ltd.
Milton Keynes UK
UKHW031808080722
405587UK00006B/860